Chinese Coins

Money in History and Society

Yu Liuliang and Yu Hong

LONG RIVER PRESS
San Francisco

Editorial Committee
Art Adviser: Yang Xin, Wang Qingzheng & Zhang Daoyi
Chief Editor: Wu Shiyu
Deputy Chief Editor: Ma Ronghua & Dai Dingjiu
Editorial Committee Members: Qian Gonglin, Lin Lanying, Zhang Debao &
Wu Shaohua

Author: Yu Liuliang & Yu Hong
Executive Editor: Dai Dingjiu & Hong Jian
Designer: Lu Quangen
Photographer: Ding Guoxing
Introduction: Zheng Tuyou
Translator: Wang Mingjie
Series Editor: Chris Robyn

ISBN 1-59265-017-1

Library of Congress Cataloging-in-Publication Data

Yu, Liuliang
Chinese coins: money in history and society / by Yu Liuliang and Yu
Hong.— 1st ed.
    p. cm.
ISBN 1-59265-017-1 (hardcover)
1. Coins, Chinese—History. 2. Coinage—China—History. 3.
Money—China—History. 4. Monetary policy—China—History. I. Yu,
Hong. II. Title.
CJ3496.Y8 2004
332.4'951—dc22

                              2003026265

Published in the United States of America by
Long River Press
3450 3rd St., #4B, San Francisco, CA 94124
www.longriverpress.com
in association with Shanghai People's Fine Arts Publishing House

Printed in China

10 9 8 7 6 5 4 3 2 1

Table of Contents

Introduction

$\mathcal{N}$umismatics is a splendid chapter of Chinese history and culture. There have existed hundreds of thousands of Chinese coins throughout history. Of the many variety of coins in China there can be found four major classifications: ancient coins, gold and silver coins, copper coins, and paper currency.

Taking the general category of ancient coins as an example, coins can be classified by materials such as bronze, copper, iron, lead, silver, tin, nickel, and even porcelain. Copper coins can further be classified as red copper, bronze, copper-nickel alloy, and brass. Cowry shells, the predecessors of coins, have been found to date from the Shang Dynasty (c. 16th-11th century B.C.). Because of the relative scarcity of naturally-occurring shells in various parts of China, iron and bronze coins were developed to emulate shells, but later evolved into other shapes common to the era: *Bu* coins (named after an ancient farming tool), *Dao* coins (named after the knife), and *Quan* coins (named after their round shape)

The shells, coins, and paper money, which could be large or small in size, heavy or light in weight, sometimes thick and sometimes thin, sometimes of good quality and sometimes of poor quality, more than anything reflected economy of their respective eras. Chinese coins are not only the reflection of the economy of a given society, but also reflect politics, military prowess, science and technology, culture, and religion. Among the various methods used to study Chinese society, coins are among the most fascinating.

1. The Rise of Chinese Currency

*S*ince the rise of commerce in the Chinese empire, the development of currency as a special means with which to conduct trade, came into being. As early as 3,000 years ago, during the Shang Dynasty, the cowry shell was used as type of currency. As commerce further developed, and the geographic boundaries of trade were widened, demand for natural shells rose, and soon shells alone were not enough to meet the demand. There then appeared imitation shells created from man-made materials. One example is the bronze shell. Since bronze shells were easily unified in size, weight and value, they were immediately recognized as being superior to natural shells. The appearance of bronze shells marked the beginning of metal coinage, which was a great step forward in the development of Chin's economy. Due to the rapid economic development in the Spring and Autumn and the Warring States Period (770-221 B.C.), there appeared various types of coins. The form of such coins imitated shapes of farming tools or items encountered in daily life.

After Qin Shi Huang Di, China's first emperor (221-207 B.C.), unified China under one ruler, he initiated a series of civil service projects, unifying roads, weights and measures, and reformed China's monetary system, utilizing a round-shaped copper coin with a square hole in its center, which was called "*ban liang qian*" or "half *liang* coin." This was the earliest reform of the monetary system in Chinese history. Such coins were elegant in appearance and were easily carried by filing a string through the holes of the coins. Coins that once before carried illegible marks, different weights, and inexplicit values, were now standardized throughout the empire. The weight and value of coins were fixed according to the needs of trade. The half *liang* coin was a milestone in the development of Chinese coinage. Since then, the pattern of a circular coin with a square hole in the center has been fixed and was adopted generation after generation until the late Qing Dynasty (1644-1911).

Business activities flourished during the Han Dynasty (206 B.C.-

A.D. 220), and the monetary system underwent yet another dramatic reform. In the 5th year of the reign of Yuan Shou of Emperor Han Wu Di (118 B.C.), the imperial house decided to strike the *wu zhu* coin (*zhu* is a unit of weight, *wu* is the designation for the number 5). It was neither very heavy nor too light. Its size and form continued until the Sui Dynasty (581-618).

The economy in China developed steadily in the Tang Dynasty (618-907) and showed and reflected the unprecedented prosperity of the time. As the largest unified empire of that time, the Tang was one of the most advanced regimes in the world. In the 4th year of the reign of Wu De of Emperor Tang Gao Zu, the *wu zhu* coin was abolished. Its replacement was called "*Kai Yuan Tong Bao*" (*Tong Bao* are two characters meaning "current coin"). It was a standard coin with a diameter of 2.5 cm, weighing about 3.5 grams, minted in imitation of the Han-dynasty's standard *wu zhu* coins. This ended the system of coins valued by weight and marked the beginning of Chinese coins with the character "bao," meaning coin. It was the second monetary revolution after Emperor Qin Shi Huang had unified Chinese currency. The Kai Yuan Tong Bao persisted for 1,300 years.

During the Song Dynasty (960-1279), both iron and copper coins were simultaneously used in the marketplace. The quantity of coins minted was remarkable. There were over a dozen Song emperors, so there were 40 to 50 types of coins with different names of their reigns. On the upper part of the reverse of the coin manufactured in the 7th year of the reign of Chun Xi of the Southern Song (1127-1279), for example, there was a Chinese character for "seven." Two years later, it was changed to a simplified form of the character for "seven." These were the so-called "coins marked with time of mint." The system of coins inscribed with a chronological mark continued until the late Song Dynasty. This method predated the coins marked with time of mint in Europe by 300 years. The Song Dynasty coins demonstrate a high degree of artistry. The characters on coins are written in various calligraphic styles. This vaulted the coin culture of China to a new, even more refined era of development. The Yuan Dynasty (1271-1368) and the Ming Dynasty (1368-1644) both promoted paper currency, and as a result, copper coins began to experience a decline.

After the mid-Ming Dynasty, silver became the main source of currency, while copper coins were used only for transactions of small value. However, it was still the main currency issued by the imperial court. During the Qing Dynasty reign of Emperor Guangxu, Zhang Zhitong, governor of Guangdong and Guangxi provinces, adopted the advanced mint technology of the West and purchased mint machines from Britain and established a mint in Guangzhou. This was the first time that Chinese coins would be struck by foreign machines, marking the third revolution in the history of the Chinese monetary system. The advanced coin minting technology of the West proved very successful during the late Qing era. Ever since then, machine-made coins have been wholly adopted in China. The machine-made coins were mainly silver and copper. Occasionally, there were coins made of gold, nickel, antimony, aluminum and even porcelain.

After the Republican revolution of 1911 in China, silver coins, the main source of currency, were replaced by paper currency. Naturally, paper money was a more advanced currency, but a lot of paper money in China was printed and issued by foreign banks. After the fall of dynastic China, foreign-printed paper money took a large share of currency circulating in the markets of China. Shaken by conflict and war for most of the 20th century, China experienced extreme currency devaluations, making most of its money nearly worthless.

It wasn't until after the establishment of the People's Republic of China in 1949 that paper money, known as Renminbi (or "People's Currency) played its full role in helping to re-establish the new Chinese economy on a domestic and global scale.

2. Coins of Various Dynasties

*E*mperor Qin Shi Huang unified and standardized China's monetary system.

By unifying competing states under the kingdom of Qin, Emperor Qin Shi Huang established a totalitarian feudal kingdom comprised of ethnic groups. This ended the chaotic era of rule by various competing warlords and kingdoms. While rule under the Qin empire could hardly be characterized as enlightened, as the rule of law was often ruthless, there nevertheless pressed forward the development of politics and economy as well as the rapid evolution of the Chinese monetary system.

After the founding of the Qin Dynasty, Emperor Qin Shi Huang stipulated that currencies would take the form of a round coin with a square hole in the center. Two Chinese characters "*ban liang*" displayed on the obverse were considered valid universal currency good throughout the realm. In fact, though the round coin with a square hole in the center was not a direct invention of Emperor Qin Shi Huang, as

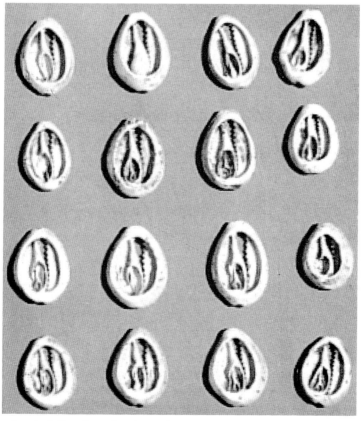

Cowrie shells – the earliest form of currency in China.

A man-made shell made of bronze.

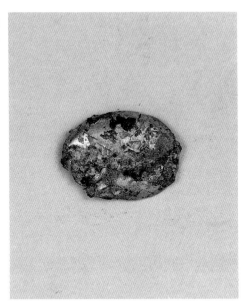

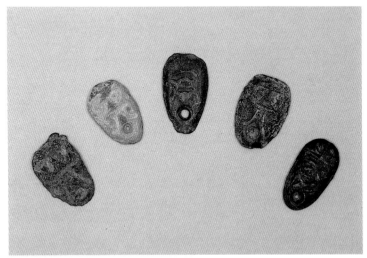

Gui Lian Qian (ghost's face coin) and *Yi Bi Qian* (ant's nose coin) are examples of the evolution of bronze currency.

other coins with similar characteristics were already in existence, notably the "*yi dao*" and "*yi hua*" coins, but their manufacture was not standardized as were the *ban liang* coins.

Chinese believed that the shape of the circle symbolized Heaven while the shape of square symbolized the earth. The ancestors of the Qin originated in the northwestern regions of China. It was there the concept of "*Tian Ming*" or "Mandate of Heaven" originated during the Spring and Autumn Period. This was the key relationship which held that a ruler must be in balance with heaven to rule effectively. An imbalance (such as flood, famine, prolonged war, etc.) would signify that a change or rule was needed. After China was unified under the Qin, the Daoist theories of opposing forces, *yin* and *yang*, were incorporated into key philosophical concepts.

Common people knew very little about natural events. Wind, rain, thunder and lightning, were all believed to be acts of the will of Heaven. The emperor was the son of Heaven and practiced Dao on behalf of Heaven. The wielding of imperial power was the Mandate of Heaven. Emperor Qin Shi Huang resorted to all types of rites and rituals, such as holding sacrificial ceremonies on Mt. Taishan, and touring many parts of the empire, to show that the Mandate of Heaven was valid and legitimate. He integrated the Mandate of Heaven and had it reflected in the pattern of the half liang coin, where the outer circular symbolized the Mandate of Heaven while the inner square the wielding of imperial power.

After currency was standardizes, and as China's economy developed, demand for quantity of coins increased. The imperial house controlled the issue and manufacturing of all coinage. The half liang coin became a symbol of imperial power. Wherever the coins travelled, imperial power prevailed. A small coin of the Qin era contains many meanings. It not only reflects the evolving nature of currency but also politics, economy, and culture of the era.

3. The Tang Dynasty: A New Age of Currency

*O*f the various types of coins whose patterns kept changing in history, the *Tong Bao* (current coins) endured for a long time and had a

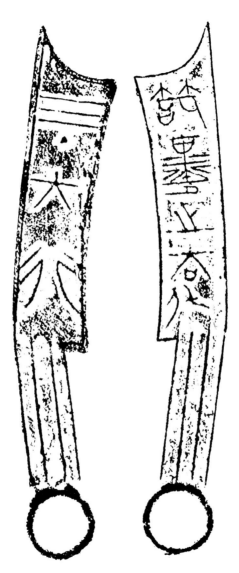

Knife-shaped currency of the Warring States Period.

Top left: Qi Ming Dao ("dao" means knife) of the Warring States Period.
Top right: From left to right: *Qi Ming Dao, Zhao Dao, Qi Ming Dao* and *Jian Shou Dao.* Warring States Period.
Bottom: Various *Bu Dao* of the Warring States Period.

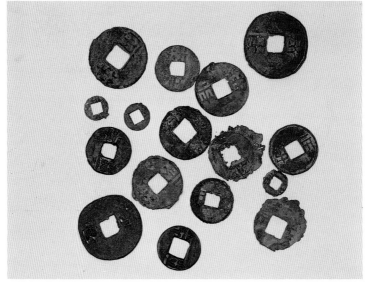

Half-*liang* coins in circulation from the Qin Dynasty to
the early Western Han.

very important position in the history of the development of Chinese currency.

The early Tang Dynasty continued to use *wu zhu* coins of the Sui Dynasty, which were small and lightweight but confusing in determining their exact value. In order to rectify the chaotic currency system, Tang Emperor Gao Zu abolished the Sui coins and began to mint "*Kai Yuan Tong Bao*," following the strict specifications of the wu zhu coins of the Western Han Dynasty in the 4th year of the reign of Wu De (A.D. 621).

Since that time, the Chinese monetary system renounced the *ban liang* coin marked with the weight of the coin. The new *tong bao* coins lasted for almost 1,300 years.

Kai Yuan Tong Bao coins inherited the Qin-dynasty pattern of outer circle and inner square. Made of copper, the coin has a diameter of 2.4 cm, weighing about 3.5 grams. It was stipulated that ten such coins would constitute one *liang*. The weight of each coin was one *qian*. A thousand coins weighed 6 *jin* (one jin equals to about a catty), 4 *liang*. This became a standard of coinage for later dynasties.

The basic form of coins of various periods of the Tang Dynasty remained unchanged. However, they might share designs or characteristics. There were designs of the moon or stars either on the obverse or reverse. The shape and the location of those designs varied. Strokes of the characters on coins were different either. There was a kind of small coin weighing only 2 grams and a big coin having a value of 10 small coins. Generally speaking, *tong bao* of the early Tang had a clear-cut outer circle and refined characters; *tong bao* of the mid-Tang had designs of the moon or stars on their reverse side; *tong bao* of the late Tang was rather coarse. The *Hui Chang Kai Yuan* coin was the representative of *Kai Yuan Tong Bao* of the late Tang.

Archaeological finds have indicated that there existed coins made of gold or silver in the early Tang. Such coins were often symbolic and were circulated only among the elite class.

4. The "Yong'an One Thousand"

*P*resent-day Daxing County in the suburbs of Beijing was called

Yong'an in the Kin Dynasty (1115-1234). Interestingly, the name Yong'an actually came from the name of the coin known as "*Yong'an Yi Qian*," used in the Five Dynasties Period (907-960). *Yi Qian* is the unit of measurement for one thousand.

According to Kin Dynasty historical records, in the first year of the reign of Zhen Yuan (1153), Prince Hai Ling chose a site in Yong'an

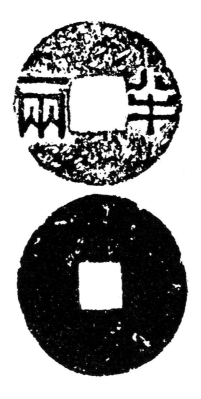

Elegant Qin dynasty half-*liang* coin
that is both thick and heavy.

to build a palace named Zhongdu. When digging ground to lay the foundation for his palace, builders found an ancient coin with characters "*Yong'an Yi Qian*." This caused quite a stir. Some officials said to the prince that this was an auspicious sign, equating Yong'an to Chang'an, the ancient capital of the prosperous Tang Dynasty. It was clearly a sign from Heaven. Prince Hai Ling was delighted. Not caring to find out when this coin had been made, he replaced the original planned name of Zhongdu with Yong'an.

In fact the coin, "*Yong'an Yi Qian*" had been a short-lived product of a bitter period of war. It had been minted under the rule of Liu Rengong and his son Liu Shouguang in the Five Dynasties Period. Both Lius were known to history as cruel warlords.

In the year 909, apart from the Five Dynasties in the north, there existed ten small kingdoms (nine in the south). The area ruled by Liu Rengong was called the Kingdom of Yan, which was too small to be included in the above ten kingdoms. In this tiny kingdom, there was a fierce power struggle between father and son. Liu Shouguang made his father's concubine his own and was thus driven away by his father. Liu Shouguang recruited many followers and took an opportunity to usurp the throne. When Shouguang got the upper hand, he imprisoned his father.

Despite their power struggle, both Liu senior and Liu junior paid a great deal of attention to minting "big coins," which were single coins carrying a high value. According to historical records, when Liu Rengong was in power, he gave orders to search for any ancient coins wherever they could be found and had them stored in vaults dug out of caves at the top of Da'an Mountain. After those coins were hidden, all workers who dug the caves were killed to prevent them from revealing their location. He had those ancient coins melted and then minted the so-called big coin "*Yong'an Yi Qian*." Before the big coins were put to use, Liu Rengong and Liu Shouguang were captured by Prince Li Chunxiang of the late Tang Dynasty and were put to death in Taiyuan. Thus the short-lived "*Yong'an Yi Qian*" came to an end.

Such coins were not minted in large quantities, nor were they widely issued. Naturally, because of their rarity they among the most highly prized coins sought by collectors today.

Kai Yuan Tong Bao of the Tang Dynasty. Note the changes to the ends of the lower horizontal stroke of the character "Yuan".

5. Tai Ping Tong Bao

Tai Ping Tong Bao means "coins in the time of great peace" A common expression among the Chinese people is their longing to live in peace. They even said "better to be a dog during a time of peace than a man in a time of turmoil". This wish was often reflected in coins.

In the reign of Tai Ping Xing Guo of the Northern Song Dynasty (960-1279), Emperor Zhao Guangyi minted the *Tai Ping Tong Bao*, which was made of copper or iron. Some people believed that the four characters on the coin was actual calligraphy of the emperor. The coins of this period found today are made of copper and iron as well as gold and silver. What was circulated in the market were copper and iron coins. Gold and silver coins were used for symbolic occasions. Coins with such characters were also minted during the Ming and Qing dynasties.

But peace was only a fond dream. Ironically, the so-called peaceful coins were all minted in periods of turmoil. Zhao Guangyi murdered his elder brother and usurped the throne. To consolidate his rule, he called his reign Tai Ping Xing Guo, which literally means a peaceful and prosperous state. He minted coins with those four characters in large quantities. But this did not help his rule. According to historical records, one of his younger brothers, and his two nephews were killed, and his sister-in-law died mysteriously. There was not a single day of peace in the imperial palace.

During the reign of Emperor Zhao Guangyi (r. 976-997), war continued without pause Zhao's armies were defeated many times in battles against the State of Liao, and people lived in misery. In his later years, a rebellion led by Wang Xiaobo and Li Shun broke out in Sichuan. Zhao Guangyi himself was the cause of all those troubles. Coins with the word "peace" could not save his reign.

Tai Ping Tong Bao coins were also minted and issued during the reign of Tian Qi of the Ming Dynasty (1368-1644), the reign of Emperor Xian Feng of the Qing Dynasty (1644-1911), as well as the rebellious army of the Little Knife Society of Shanghai. Their purpose was the same: seeking and keeping peace. These coins with common characteristics have a history of over 3,000 years, making them truly fascinating in how they reflect both change and continuity in Chinese society.

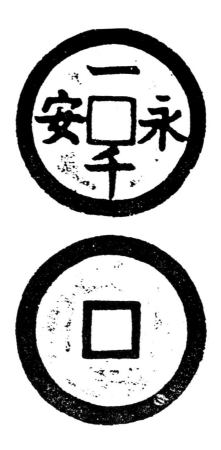

Yong'an Yi Qian, or Yong'an One Thousand, of the Five Dynasties and Ten Kingdoms.

Apart from *Yong'an Yi Qian*, the Five Dynasties and Ten Kingdoms also minted many precious coins such as *Yong Long* iron coin, *Kai Yuan* lead coins, and *Yong Tong Quan Huo* iron coins.

6. A Mediocre Emperor, An Expert of Coinage

*E*mperor Hui Zong of the Northern Song Dynasty created a system of calligraphy known as "*Shou Jin Ti*" or "thin metallic style." On the obverse of a large number of extant coins minted in the Northern Song, we can see his vigorous and powerful characters.

Hui Zong succeeded his elder brother and became the emperor. He was particularly fond of calligraphy and art. During the 26 years of his reign, he personally inscribed and crafted the *Chong Ning Tong Bao, Da Guan Tong Bao*, and *Xuan He Tong Bao* coins. Those in later generations called coins with his writing the "coins of imperial calligraphy."

Copper coins known as *Chong Ning Tong Bao* with imperial calligraphy were struck in *xiao ping* and ten-cash coins. The former were common, basic denomination coins while the latter had a value 10 times that of the former. There were various editions of the ten-cash coin, which were meticulously minted by craftsmen under the personal guidance of Emperor Hui Zong. The characters inscribed on the obverse of coins by the emperor display vigorous strokes and an elegant structure. It can be called one of the wonders of coinage in ancient China.

There were also coins known as *Da Guan Tong Bao*, which were valued at double, triple, and quintuple the base *xiao ping* currency. In the eyes of collectors, of all coins with Emperor Hui Zong's calligraphy, the best is the *Chong Ning Tong Bao*, with the *Da Guan Tong Bao* close behind.

Iron coins with the imperial calligraphy include the double-value *Chong Ning Tong Bao*, the *xiao ping* and double value *Da Guan Tong Bao*, *Xuan He Tong Bao* with a character "*shan*" on the reverse, some having a large "*shan*" and some having a small "*shan*." Others have the character close to the outer circle, some having the character close to the central square.

During the reign of Song Emperor Da Guan, the four characters on the obverse of the large silver coin were written in a clockwise way instead of usual way of top, bottom, right and left. Such coins were used as gifts in the imperial court of the Song Dynasty, and are extremely rare. During the reign of Zheng He, apart from coins with characters written in official script and seal script, there were also various types of *xiao ping* coins with characters written in regular script.

When it came to managing state affairs, Emperor Hui Zong was mediocre at best. But he paid great attention to the quality and technology of coinage, and no emperor in Chinese history could match him in this regard. No wonder, people of later generations called him a prominent artist but not a qualified ruler.

7. The Origin of "*Zhao Na Xin Bao*"

*T*here once existed a coin that was able to cause enemy troops to lay down their arms. Such a magic coin was called "*Zhao Na Xin Bao*," or

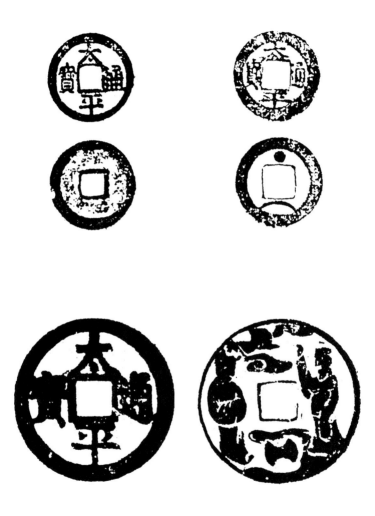

Top left: Tai Ping Tong Bao minted in the Northern Song Dynasty.
Top right: Tai Ping Tong Bao minted by the rebellious army of the Shanghai Little Knife Society.
Bottom: Tai Ping Tong Bao minted in the Ming Dynasty.

"Trust Token for Recruits," invented by a general named Liu Guangshi.

In the summer of 1311, the Southern Song army and the troops of the Kingdom of Kin were locked in a fierce fight. As they were evenly matched in strength, they were in a stalemate, facing each other across the Yangtze River. At dawn each morning there would appear some Kin troops who had ferried themselves across the river and went to the barracks of the Southern Song troops. There they would fish out some coins from their pockets and showed them to the Southern Song soldiers. The Song soldiers became very friendly at the sight of these coins and entertained the Kin troops in their barracks. What kind of coins did the Kin troops carry? Why were the Southern Song soldiers delighted to see those enemies with such coins? In fact, those coins were not ordinary coins but special tokens minted by General Liu Shiguang.

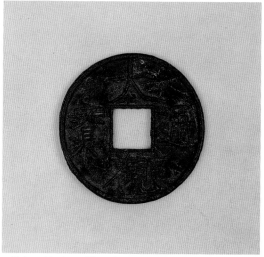

Coin with the calligraphy of Emperor Hui
Zong of the Song Dynasty.

A 50x value coin minted under Emperor Hui Zong.

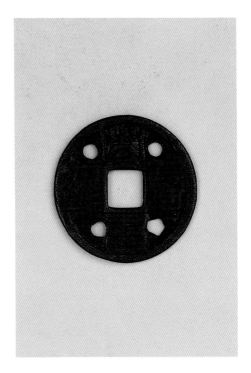

In the course of the war, Liu had learned that many Kin troops had been conscripted by force. They were homesick and hated the war. When Liu captured enemy soldiers, he did not kill or imprison them. Instead he would persuade them to surrender. Then he would give a banquet to send them back home, and offered them some copper tokens. Those tokens had been stricken at the order of General Liu. Such tokens were made of gold, silver, and copper. On the obverse of the token there were four Chinese characters "*Zhao Na Xin Bao*," meaning "trust token for recruits." On the reverse of the token there was a character "*shi*" (meaning "envoy") over the square hole. The Kin soldiers returned to their own barracks and gave out those tokens to those who wished to surrender. Any Kin soldier who could produce such a token to the Southern Song troops would be treated with hospitality. Sure enough, this method worked. More and more Kin soldiers joined the Song troops in this way. Before long, more than 20,000 Kin soldiers of Nüzhen, Qidan and Han origin surrendered and were organized into two new armies, which played a very important role in later battles. Finally, the Kin army was defeated.

A coin-like token defeated thousands of enemy troops. Ever since that time, the "*Zhao Na Xin Bao*" became known far and wide throughout the empire. Unfortunately, tokens minted during the war were very limited in quantity, and later became widely scattered. It is extremely rare to see such tokens today, as they are now considered priceless historical treasures.

8. A Coin Museum at the Riverbed in Gaoyou

*W*hen portions of the Grand Canal were widened in July 1985, a large number of ancient coins were discovered at the riverbed of the section in Gaoyou, Jiangsu province. The find consisted of various editions of iron coins minted during the Southern Song. There were so many varieties and such great quantities that the find was described as a "museum of coins."

Gaoyou is 40 miles to the north of Yangzhou City. During the reign of Jin Emperor Yin Zheng, a common military policy was to "build high (*gao*) platforms to establish lookout posts (*you*).

Gaoyou is a trove of cultural relics either on the ground or under the ground. There are Zhoudun ruins dating from the Shang and Zhou dynasties; the mausoleum of King Guang Ling of the Western Han; the Zhengguo Temple Pagoda of the Tang; the post stations of Yucheng of the Ming. Pu Songling, a noted writer of the Qing Dynasty once commented, "Gaoyou is one of the best-known places for cultural relics."

The location where the trove of coins was unearthed is to the west of the imperial docks at Gaoyou. Iron coins had been discovered twice in this area already. The first time was during the reign of Emperor Jia Qing, and the second time was in 1957 when the new Great Canal was built. Also unearthed were copper coins and metal

Trust Token for Recruits of the Southern Song Dynasty.

objects totalling several tons.

A close look at these iron coins would reveal a rich set of cultural elements in those coins. They belonged to the State of Chu, Western Han, Eastern Han, Sui, Tang, Latter Han, Latter Zhou, Former Shu, Southern Tang, Song, Jin, Yuan, Da Zhou, Ming, and Qing dynasties, spanning a period of more than 2,000 years. The coins are made of copper, iron, lead, silver, etc. They were coins used in the market or coins used as tokens of auspiciousness or as gifts. According to the Yangzhou Coin Society, there are almost 800 types of iron coins of the Southern Song if divided by editions, mint supervisory boards, and date of minting.

Many types of coins unearthed in Gaoyou had not been previously seen or heard of in history. This has enriched and filled some gaps of the currency history of China. The discovery of iron coins in large quantity has also proved the historical fact that iron coins were widely used in Huainan (the region between the Huai River and the Yangtze River in central Anhui Province), and Huaibei (the region north of the Huai River in northern Anhui Province), as well as confirming the reliability of certain historical records.

These coins are indicative of the high level of coin manufacturing in the Southern Song. Moreover, it is also significant in the study of the economic and monetary system of the Southern Song, and the history of the region of Gaoyou and Yangzhou. The discovery has provided precious materials for the study of circulation of iron coins in the Southern Song as well as history of ancient Chinese coinage.

9. A Monetary Slip Worth 15,000 RMB

*A*part from striking iron coins in large quantities, the Southern Song also minted a short-lived, uniquely shaped currency known as the Lin'an Prefecture Monetary Slip. Though short-lived, there had been nothing like it before nor anything similar to it since. When discussing ancient coins in China, its inclusion is of paramount significance.

The money slop was made of copper or lead in a vertical rectangular shape. On the top there is a round hole, which was used for string to be passed through. The legend on its obverse contains five

Iron coins unearthed in Gaoyou.

characters meaning "valid in Lin'an Prefecture" in regular script. The value of each copper slip is marked on the reverse indicating a multiple of 200, 300, or 500 times the base value. The lead slip marks the value of 10 or 40 above base value.

According to *History of the Song Dynasty,* since the Northern Song was wiped out by the Kin, Emperor Song Zong fled south and finally ended up in the area of Hangzhou. In 1129, the third year of the reign of Jian Yan of Emperor Gao Zong, this region was changed to Lin'an Prefecture. For more than 150 years, the name of Lin'an remained unchanged. Soon after, Lin'an became the capital of the Southern Song.

Compared with the former Northern Song, the strength of the Southern Song was even weaker. In the face of the pressure from the Kin and Mongols in the north, the financial situation of the Southern Song deteriorated into a major crisis towards its later years. One of the emergency measures was to mint large-valued monetary slips.

However, it was only a temporary remedial method. As such slips were not very convenient, they soon stopped circulating. According to History of the Song Dynasty, in 1265, in the seventh month of the first year of the reign of Xian Chun, the use of money slips was banned.

As monetary slips marked with characters "valid in Lin'an Prefecture" lasted only for a short period of time, not many survive to this day. Because of its unique shape, such monetary slips have become favorites of coin collectors. In the Catalogue of Chinese Ancient Coins, published by Xinjiang Publishing House in 1996, a Southern Song money slip marked with the value of 200 was priced at RMB 15,000 (about US$2,000).

10. Ethnic Coins of the Yuan Dynasty

*T*he Yuan (or Mongol) Dynasty (1271-1368), came to usurp the Song. They adopted paper money for use in trade. Comparatively speaking, not many coins were minted in the Yuan period. Those coins that were minted carried Han Chinese characters or even Mongolian script, which is often called Phags-pa. The language was named after Phags-

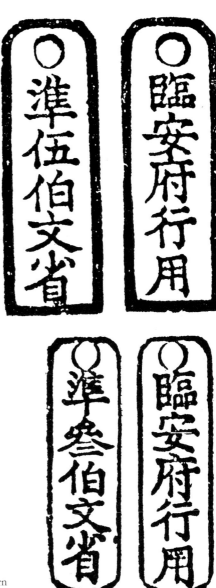

Currency slips of the Southern
Song Dynasty.

pa (1235-1280), leader of Tibetan Lamaism, who created the new Mongolian characters. It was the first time in Chinese history that coins had borne characters of another ethnic (non-Han) group.

The Mongolian ethnic group was an ancient nomadic nationality in the north of China. Before Phags-pa script, the Mongols had had no written script of their own. When Genghis Khan founded the Kingdom of Mongolia, he initially adopted Tibetan language, but written in Huihu script. The Huihu had also been a nomadic nationality in ancient China. By the time of the reign of his grandson Kublai Khan, Phags-pa script was adopted.

The meaning of Phags-pa in Tibetan language is equivalent to that of "saint." Phags-pa was said to be able to recite tens of thousand scriptures and understood their basic meanings when he was only seven years old. He was known as a sacred infant genius. In 1253, he was summoned by Kublai to work for him and was held in high esteem. When Kublai ascended the throne in 1260, Phags-pa was venerated as the Master of the State and appointed as the first minister in charge of affairs related to Tibet and Buddhism. He was also requested to create a new system of script and in 1269 it was completed. Kublai issued a decree to adopt the new script as one of the official scripts of the Yuan Dynasty, which could be used together with other scripts, including Han script. The Phags-pa script was based on phonetic alphabet created on the basis of the Tibetan script and is comprised of 41 letters.

The Yuan dynasty coins with legends of Phags-pa characters include *Zhi Yuan Tong Bao*, valid from the reign of Emperor Shi Zu to the reign of Yuan Nian; *Yuan Zhen Tong Bao* and *Da De Tong Bao*, valid from the reign of Yuan Zhen to the reign of Da De; *Da Yuan Tong Bao*, valid from the reign of Wu Zong to the reign of Da Nian, which is relatively thick and heavy and issued in a large quantity. Each of the latter was worth ten basic *Zhi Da Tong Bao* with Chinese characters.

There was a variety of coins minted during the reign of Zhi Zhen of Emperor Yuan Shun. On the obverse of those coins there are Chinese characters "*Zhi Zheng Tong Bao.*" Over the hole of the reverse, there is time of mint in Phags-pa script. On some coins, there are both Chinese and Phags-pa script indicating value on the reverse. Also found are lead coins with Chinese character indicating a value of

Coins with Phags-pa characters of the Yuan Dynasty.

25 on the obverse and Phags-pa script meaning "power" on the reverse. Such coins are extremely rare.

11. Coinage of Peasant Uprisings

$\mathcal{T}$he rulers of the Yuan led a debauched life and levied heavy taxes on the population. There were numerous peasant revolts during the late Yuan Dynasty. The revolts stretched from the upper reaches of the Yellow River, Huai River, and Yangtze River in China's hinterland. Many of these breakaway regions established their own seats of political power and even minted their own currency. The Yuan Dynasty was quickly approaching its end. This is a significant page in the history of ancient coinage.

The Red Scarf Army led by Liu Futong and Han Shantong was the main force of the peasant uprisings during the late Yuan Dynasty. After Han Shantong was arrested and executed, Liu Futong attacked and took Runing, Xizhou, and Guangzhou. At its height Liu's army consisted of more than 100,000 troops. In 1355, Liu Futong invited Han Shantong's son Han Lin'er to come out of exile to be the emperor. A provisional capital was established in Bozhou and the name of the kingdom was called Great Song. The first reign period was named Long Feng. So coins minted at that time had the inscription of "*Long Feng Tong Bao*," which were circulated in the vicinity of Huaisi. There were coins of *xiao ping* (base currency), as well as coins of double and triple valuation. Due to internal power struggles, however, the Great Song failed. In 1366, Han Lin'er drowned when attempting to cross a river at Guabu. Coins minted during this period have become highly treasured since when minted they were both thick and heavy and inscribed with powerful calligraphy.

While Liu Futong started the uprising in Yingzhou, another rebellion took place in the eighth month of 1351 in Qizhou, Hubei Province. The armed force, led by Peng Yinyu and Xu Shouhui, had been active for a long time in the area of the Yangtze River and Huai River. In the tenth month, the uprising took Qishui and set up a kingdom named Tian Wan. The name of the first reign was called Zhi Ping, and Xu Shouhui was chosen to be the emperor. In 1356, the capital was moved to Hanyang and the reign was changed to Taiping. In 1358, it was changed again to Tian Qi. Coins minted in this period had the characters "*Tian Qi Tong Bao*" and consisted of three types: *xiao ping* (base currency), double, and triple valuation. The triple value

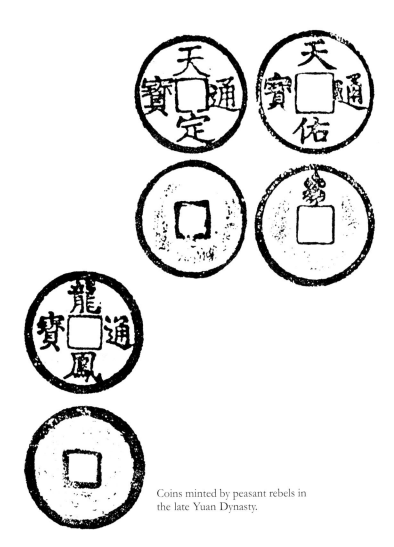

Coins minted by peasant rebels in the late Yuan Dynasty.

coin had characters in seal script but had no words on the reverse. In 1359, the capital was moved to Jiangzhou and the reign title was changed to Tian Ding, hence the *"Tian Ding Tong Bao,"* which continued with the same currency denomination.

In 1360, Chen Youliang seized power and proclaimed himself emperor. The name of the kingdom was changed to Han and the reign was called Da Yi. Coins minted under the new ruler were called *"Da Yi Tong Bao,"* which carried the same value as the *Tian Ding Tong Bao.*

Apart from the above two, a man named Zhang Shicheng led a revolt in 1353 in Gaoyou. Zhang's forces defeated the Yuan army and set up a capital at Gaoyou.

He called the new regime Da Zhou. The first reign title was called Tian You. Zhang destroyed Buddhist statues made of copper and used them to mint *"Tian You Tong Bao,"* or which there were four types: base, double, triple, and quintuple value.

The obverse had characters in regular script while the reverse were marked with numerical markings for one, two, three and five in seal script to indicate value. These coins were circulated in western Zhejiang, in the reaches of the Huai River, including the cities of Yangzhou, Suzhou, and Changzhou.

Peasant uprisings during the late Yuan Dynasty brought about a number of coins. Since these new regimes were, for the most part, short-lived, the coins surviving today are rare and highly sought after. It is difficult if not outright impossible to have a complete collection of coins minted during the peasant rebellions of the late Yuan. This is especially true of the double-value *Tian Qi Tong Bao* minted by Xu Shouhui, of which only two such coins have been found to date.

12. Zhu Yuanzhang and *Da Zhong Tong Bao*

Social chaos in the late Yuan Dynasty caused serious damage to the economy. The paper money system of the Yuan collapsed and coins soon replaced them in the marketplace. The regimes established by rebellious peasants minted coins on their own, such as the *Long Feng Tong Bao* by Han Lin' e r, *Tian Qi Tong Bao* and *Tian Ding Tong Bao* by Xu

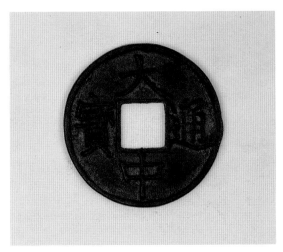

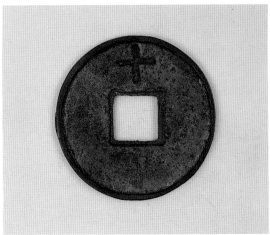

Da Zhong Tong Bao minted by Emperor Zhu Yuanzhang. Ming Dynasty.

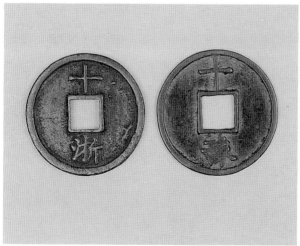

Hong Wu Tong Bao marked with mint of origin. Early Ming Dynasty.

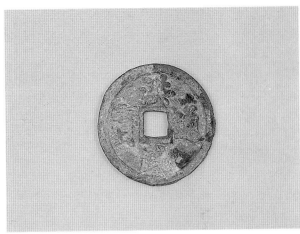

Hong Wu Tong Bao marked with weight minted by Zhu
Yuanzhang. Ming Dynasty.

Shouhui, *Tian You Tong Bao* by Zhang Shicheng, *Da Yi Tong Bao* by Chen Youliang, *Tian Tong Tong Bao* by Yu Zhen and *Da Zhong Tong Bao* by Zhu Yuanzhang. The above six anti-Yuan rebellious movements manufactured coins according to their own systems.

Of the above six powers, Zhu Yuanzhang was the most successful as far as coinage is concerned. At first, Zhu had been a subordinate of Han Lin'er. Zhu led his army to victory in many battles. Soon he became a favorite of Han Lin'er and was bestowed the title "State Lord Wu." Though there already existed Han's *Long Feng Tong Bao*, Zhu was thus not allowed to strike any other coins. Zhu, however, was unwilling to be knuckled under and had his own way about coin use in the marketplace. While assisting Han in manufacturing coins, Zhu also gave consent for people to continuously use Yuan currency called *jiao chao*. Furthermore, he stimulated the use of such coins by stipulating that one *liang* of *jiao chao* was worth 40 *Long Feng Tong Bao*, while ten *liang* of *jiao chao* was worth 100! To complement this practice, he established the Baoyuan Mint in Yingtian Prefecture and began to strike coins called *Da Zhong Tong Bao*, which could be used along with other coins.

When Zhu defeated Chen Youliang in the 24th year of the reign of Zhi Yuan, Zhu believed that it was high time to establish another mint. Shortly thereafter, the Baoquan Mint in Jiangxi was formed and began producing *Da Zhong Tong Bao* on a large scale.

Copper coins circulating in the late Yuan Dynasty were usually divided in three mjor denominations: *xiao ping* (base value), double, and triple value. In certain places, there were four denominations. *Da Zhong Tong Bao* could be classified in five denominations: *xiao ping*, 2x, 3x, 5x, and 10x base value. Zhu issued coins with the mint of origin displayed. Few such coins survive today. Examples are *Da Zhong* coins with characters *E, Guang* and *Ji* on the reverse. The *Da Zhong* series are perhaps the rarest of all coins of this era.

In 1368, Zhu Yuanzhang ascended the throne and formally established the Ming Dynasty. His first reign was called Hong Wu. So from then on, he minted *Hong Wu Tong Bao*, and *Da Zhong Tong Bao* came to an end.

Paper currency was also printed during the Ming Dynasty, however, it did not replace the minting of coins.

13. Coins of the Ming Dynasty

The Ming Dynasty (1368-1644) lasted for 276 years and had 17 emperors. Of eleven emperors from Tai Zu to Wu Zong, coins were minted only during the reigns of Hong Wu, Yong Le, Xuan De, and Hong Zhi. Seven emperors did not care to manufacture coins during their reigns. One of the means for Emperor Zhu Yuanzhang to seize power was in the manufacture of coins. But when he became the first Ming emperor, he ordered a stoppage to coin minting and actively resumed the printing of paper money. This was because he realized copper coins were too costly to mint and took a great deal of man-power. By comparison, it was much easier to print paper money.

The reason for the failure of paper money during the Yuan was a lack of economic strength and poor administration. When Emperor Zhu Yuanzhang formally issued *Da Ming Bao Chao* (literally: "current paper money of the Great Ming,") he paid special attention to those issues. He stipulated that any one who made counterfeit paper currency would be executed, and that anyone who reported an act of genuine counterfeiting would be awarded 250 taels of silver as well as all of the property confiscated from the guilty party. In the early Ming Dynasty, as society became peaceful, development of the economy remained stable. This provided a good environment for the circulation of paper money.

One aspect worth noting is that all coins minted by the Ming no longer bear the character "yuan," used to denote money, and which had appeared on all coins since the Tang Dynasty. The character would later reappear on coins made during the early 20th century, but why did they disappear during the Ming? There are two explanations: In a feudal society, the name of the emperor was not to be spoken or even read by the common people, and therefore all efforts were made to avoid it completely. Since "yuan" is synonymous with the name Zhu Yuanzhang, the name of the Emperor, it was not reproduced in any way on coinage. The other explanation is an obvious one: the rulers of the Ming hated to see the any mention of "Yuan," which of course was the name of the dynasty which had just been overthrown.

So when the Yuan Dynasty ended, any similar-sounding character could not possibly be used for coins of the new regime. During the entire span of the Ming Dynasty, the word "*Yuan*" never appeared on coins again.

Xi Wang Shang Gong made of gold minted by Zhang Xianzhong, also known as King Xi (or *Xi Wang*).

14. Coins as Medals

*I*n ancient China, the earliest awards for those who made great contributions to the empire were often presented in the form of ceremonial coins.

As early as the Tang Dynasty, the principal currency, *Kai Yuan Tong Bao*, was often used by the imperial court as an award bestowed to military leaders, nobility, and valued retainers of the imperial household. Such coins were made of gold, silver or gold-gilt. Historical records even record how such coins were bestowed during festivals.

Such coin awards also appeared during the Song Dynasty. Many coins made of gold and silver of the Song have been excavated. Gold coins include *Tai Ping Tong Bao, Xuan He Tong Bao* and *Qian Long Tong Bao*. Silver coins include *Tai Ping Tong Bao, Da Guan Tong Bao, Zheng He Tong Bao, Xuan He Yuan Bao, Bao He Tong Bao*, and *Qing Yuan Tong Bao*. All are very rare.

Rebellious peasant armies also minted their own ceremonial. One example is the coin with the characters "*Xi Wang Shang Gong*," signifying a ceremonial coin bestowed by King Xi Wang, and minted under the rule of Zhang Xianzhong of the late Ming Dynasty.

Zhang was a famous leader of a peasant uprising. In 1634, he proclaimed himself Great King Xi Wang. The next year, he took Chengdu and Sichuan and proclaimed himself emperor. His kingdom, located in Chengdu, was named Da Xi and the title of the reign Da Shun. Zhang minted the *Da Shun Tong Bao* for trading, and coins of gold, silver and copper with the characters *Xi Wang Shang Gong* for use as ceremonial coins. Many *Da Shun Tong Bao* have been handed down through the generations since, comparatively speaking, they were minted in large quantities. The ceremonial or award coins are extremely rare, particularly the coins made of gold and silver, since they were minted in very limited numbers.

Examples of *Chong Zhen Tong Bao*.

15. Confusing Coins Minted Under Emperor Chong Zhen

*A*fter a period of prosperity, the Chinese economy declined again in the late Ming Dynasty. The Ming paper money became worthless as it lacked popular support. Again, coins reappeared and the stage was set for an economic revival.

To cope with the situation, Emperor Chong Zhen allowed mints throughout the empire to make coins freely. Since there were no unified rules or standards, coins made in different mints were altogether different in size and were known by different names. The characters on the reverse of the coins, which had Chong Zhen Tong Bao, on the obverse, also varied. It was a very confusing system for the average person to understand. It also provides a fascinating mystery for coin lovers and collectors of today.

Roughly, such coins can be divided into six types.

The first type has patterns on the reverse of coins, including designs of stars, the sun, the moon, galloping horse, etc. But horse and the moon are rare to see.

The second type has time of mint marked on the reverse of coins, namely, *Jia, Yi, Bing, Ding, Wu, Ji, Geng* (meaning one, two, three, four, five, six, seven), indicating each year from the 7th year to the 13th year of the reign of Chong Zhen. But the coins with *Ding* and *Geng* are especially rare.

The third type has the weight marked on the reverse of coins, including more than ten variants such as *Yi Fen* (base value), *Jiu Yi Fen, Xin Qian, Chong Yi Fen, Ba Fen, Ba, Ba*. Here, Chong refers to the city of Chongqing, Hu, the ministry of revenue, Jiu and Xin refer to the names of mints. Among these coins, coins with *Xin Qian* and coins with *Yi Fen* in a vertical order on the left of the reverse are most rare.

The fourth type has the name of mint administrative boards on the reverse of the coins. There are ten such boards, indicating on the reverse of coins by characters of *Hu, Gong, Xin, Jiu, Jiu, Hujiu, Bing, Ju, Jing* and *Yuan*. Coins with characters of *Jiu, Jing, Bing* and *Yuan* are among the rarest.

The fifth type has the name of places of mint marked on the

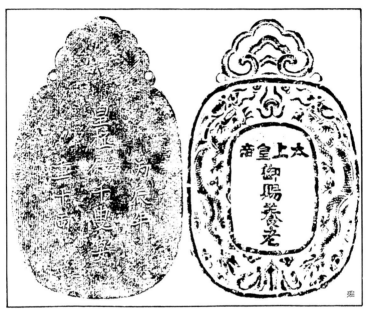

A silver slip used for the *Banquet of a Thousand Elders*

reverse of coins. There are altogether 16 places, namely, *Ying, Jia, Jia, Ning, Chong, Hu, Zhong, Gui, Guang, Yu, Taiping, Fu, Gong, E, Qing* and *Jiang*. Coins with *Jia, Ning* and *Yu* are rare. To date, the exact geographic locations of certain places of mint are still not known.

The sixth type has the characters like *Guan, Chi, Zhi, Feng Zhi, Zhi, Xing*. The first five all mean "minted at the order of the imperial edict" and the last one means "acting on the imperial edict." Coins with *Zhi, Zhi* and *Xing* are very rare.

Apart from the above six types, there are also coins with characters *Qing Zhong, Ji, He, Dao*. Their meanings—in the context of the coins on which they appear—are still unknown. As far as size is concerned, there are both "broad outer circle" and "narrow outer circle." Collectors of Chinese coins have established worldwide networks in order to help solve these puzzling historical issues.

16. Silver Slips for the Banquet of A Thousand Elders

*B*oth Emperor Kang Xi and Emperor Qian Long of the Qing Dynasty invited, in their respective reigns, a large number of high-ranking officials and generals to banquets held in the imperial palace. On each occasion, a "thousand elders" attended such banquets. To remember the event, each attendee was given a silver slip which weighed approximately 10 taels. Shaped roughly in an oval, the slip has four characters "*Yu Chi Yang Lao*," (literally "bestowed by the emperor to wish you a long life") in bas-relief, surrounded by a design of the "two dragons playing a pearl." This is also known as "Silver Slip for the Banquet of A Thousand Elders." The slip is 14 cm in height and 9 cm in width.

In 1736, the first year of the reign of Emperor Qianlong, the emperor announced to his ministers that he would rule for 60 years and then pass the throne to his son. Sure enough, in 1796, exactly 60 years later, Qian Long held a grand ceremony and handed over the power to his son Liu Zong (also known as Emperor Jia Qing).

17. The Origin of Arhat Coins

Since the Qing Dynasty was the last of China's dynasties—extending into the 20th century, many of its coins have been handed down and can be studied and collected to this day. With the increasing interest and availability in Qing-era coins, there have appeared many stories about popular coins in China's past. The story of Arhat coins is one example.

The Arhat coin is regarded as a folk treasure. It is often given as a special gift to dear friends and loved ones on the eve Chinese New Year. The Arhat coin is to be placed at the bottom of a trunk for a daughter when she is married. Others believe that there is gold contained within Arhat coins and try to extract gold by melting them. The power of the Arhat coin has been much exaggerated.

There are many folktales about the origin of Arhat coins. In the

Arhat coins.

early 16th century, the Qing Emperor Kang Xi sent troops to suppress insurrections in Tibet via Qinghai and Sichuan. On their way there, due to lack of pay and provisions for soldiers, the army commander had to turn to Buddhist temples to borrow copper in order to make coins. In fear, the monks had to hand over many copper statues of Arhats, or religious figures. To meet the demand, the monks had to give up 18 statues of Arhats. Coins made from their copper shone with the light of gold.

More than 50 years ago, researchers looked into the origins of Arhat coins. Through a Buddhist abbot named Lang Wu, researchers learned of the Jingsi Temple in Hangzhou.

The Jingsi Temple in Hangzhou was to be renovated during the reign of Qing Emperor Dao Guang. As preparation were under way, a resident monk suddenly discovered a string of brand new coins inside a statue of an Arhat. He untied the string and found that they were all quality coins minted on the occasion of the 60th birthday of the Emperor Kang Xi. Inscriptions on such coins are slightly different than those of other coins of the same period: they were called *Wan Shou* coins at that time (and are now known simply as Arhat coins.) The string of coins was actually hidden there by a Buddhist benefactor of the statue, probably during the reign of Kang Xi or Yong Zheng. Such practice had in fact started in the Yuan Dynasty. The head monk of the Jingsi Temple claimed that anyone who possessed such a coin would be protected by the Arhats and would live a long life. The coin, furthermore, would expel all evil spirits.

This pronouncement attracted a large number of Buddhist devotees and benefactors, who wished to make donations simply to receive an Arhat coin. Since that time, the coins were referred to as Arhat coins, and the original name, *Wan Shou*, was gradually forgotten. This is how the name of Arhat coin was originated.

In fact, the Arhat coins we see today are largely ceremonial and were minted many times and in large quantities in recent history. The coins truly minted from copper are rare. It was in the 3rd month of the year 1713, that the coins commemorating the 60th birthday of Emperor Kangxi were minted under the Baoquan Board of the Ministry of Revenue in Beijing at the order of the imperial house. Those little copper coins all have wide outer circle, are of good quality, glossy

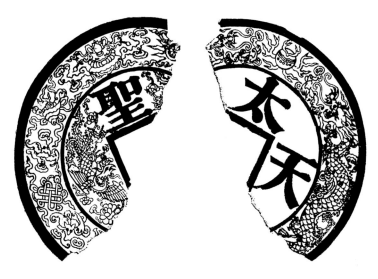

The heaviest coin in Chinese history is the *hua qian*, or floral coin.

and smooth. On the reverse, there are scripts in Manchurian, a translation of Baoquan.

Folktales have shrouded the coins with mystery. Gradually, those ordinary coins, now called Arhat coins, have become the theme of many stories, some of which have even been adopted for stage performance.

18. Coins of the Taiping Heavenly Kingdom

*A*ncient Chinese coins have drawn more and more attention from researchers and collectors. Which coin is the largest in size? Which coin is the heaviest in weight? Not too many people know all the questions. In a book entitled Coins of the Taiping Heavenly Kingdom (1851-1864) compiled by Ma Dingxiang can be found perhaps the largest coin in terms of size. What was found, was unfortunately only half a piece of a larger coin called "*hua qian*." This relic is now housed in Hunan Museum in Changsha. It has a diameter of 33.5 cm and a thickness of 0.8 cm. The recovered piece weighs 2,170 grams (about 4.8 lbs). Researchers have determined that the whole coin would be as large as a small basin and weigh about 4,500 grams (about 10 lbs).

In a publication entitled *Labor Daily* from the former Soviet Union, it was reported that a copper coin exhibited in Uzbek Nationality Cultural Museum in Samarqand was as large as a plate for teacups and with a weight of 919 grams. At the time it was called heaviest copper coin. But compared to the *Taiping Hua Qian*, it is only one fifth the weight! Compared with the current one-yuan coin, the *Hua Qian* is 759 times heavier and more than 170 times larger!

The *Taiping Hua Qian* is made of copper and gold gilt. There are only two characters depicted, *Tai* and *Tian*, which represent two out of the four characters: *Tai Ping Tian Guo* meaning Taiping (Great Peace) Heavenly Kingdom, on the obverse.

The wide outer circle of the coin is carved with a pattern of two dragons playing with a pearl. On the reverse, there is only one character "*Sheng*" meaning sacred, surrounded by two phoenixes. The broad outer circle is covered by a design of the Eight Treasures. The strokes of those characters are both vigorous and squared. The de-

The Taiping Rebellion of the mid 1800s took place during the reign of Emperor Xian Feng of the Qing Dynasty, one of the most chaotic periods of late Imperial China.

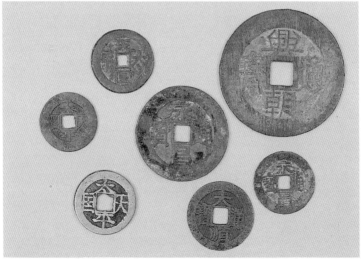

Coins minted by the Taiping rebels.

Coins minted by the
Taiping rebels.

ID Tokens of the Heaven and Earth Society.

ID Tokens of the Heaven and Earth Society.

signs are exquisite and vivid. The coin is refined and of good quality. This indicates that the coin manufacturing technology during the era of the Taiping Heavenly Kingdom was very high.

Such coins were not made for trade. The coin was used on the occasion of the launch of a mint furnace or for ceremonial use. It was mainly used as a "ritual coin." The *Hua Qian* in the Hunan Museum is a priceless treasure as well as a most important relic. It is indeed the largest and the heaviest coin in Chinese history.

19. Coins and Secret Societies

*I*n China today, the rapid growth of social clubs and club memberships seems to be a new measurement of social status. Few people have seen the earliest "memberships" of secret societies in imperial China. At the time, most activities were concerned with opposing the reigning dynasty. The first such membership in a secret society shared some kinship with coins.

The earliest membership pass looks like a coin. It was called "*Xin Hao Qian*" or ID Token, issued by an organization known as Tian Di Hui, or Heaven and Earth Society. In 1858, intolerant of opposition of the Qing Dynasty, six men including Zhao Qi, Zhou Rong of Qiancang Town of Pingyang County in Zhejiang Province formed a secret organization called the Coin Group based in Beishan Temple, and joined the Heaven and Earth Society with an aim to overthrow the Qing Dynasty. The society formulated its rules, requesting that society members must abide by those rules and instructions of the leaders.

The *Xin Hao Qian*, made of copper, is 37 mm in diameter and weighs about 19 grams. On the front of the token there are four characters "*Jin Qian Yi Ji*". On the left and right sides of the back, each has a design of two partially overlapped rhombus designs. The four rhombuses were said to signify unity of people from all corners. There are also tokens, one size larger, which bear the characters *Li, Tian, Di* over the square-shaped hole. They were specially made for leaders of the society.

The society was finally wiped out by the Qing government due to shortage of men and funds. Even the membership tokens were banned and destroyed. Therefore, today only a few such coins are kept in museums of Shanghai and Jilin. Tokens with characters for leaders are extremely rare.

20. Chinese *Hua Qian*

*A*ncient Chinese coins have a history of over 3,000 years. Apart from the large quantity of circulating coins, there have also existed coins not used for trade, minted either by official furnaces or private furnaces. Some coins have designs and scripts, others bear designs only. The latter are known simply as *hua qian*, literally, floral coins.

Chinese *hua qian* are also called "*Yan Sheng Qian*"; "*Yan*" means something disgusting or a curse while "*sheng*" means to triumph over or subdue.

Examples of *hua qian*.

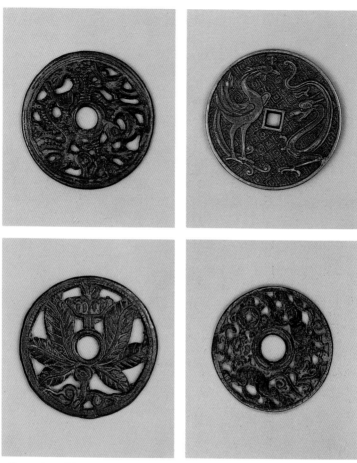

Examples of *hua qian*.

Examples of *hua qian*.

The earliest *Yan Sheng Qian* was a superstitious token in the shape of a coin. Apart from scripts, it has borne all manner of designs. Later, the utility of such tokens grew wider. Coin collectors gave a general term "*hua qian*" to refer to all such coins. These include coins signifying longevity, awards, honor or decoration, riddles, astrological signs, curses, oracles, temples, or hell. Though sometimes they might be mixed with coins for trade, they were actually manifestation of traditions in culture, entertainment, religion, myth, local custom, and way of life, etc. Loved by people, they were handed down generation to generation. Even when the society entered into a modern age, they continued to play their role and develop in their own way.

In recent years, there have appeared many types of souvenir badges which are in fact an evolution of *Hua Qian*. Many new varieties have become objects for collectors and continue to grow more popular. In Shanghai alone, for example, there is a large copper badge club, and it is common to see people standing in long lines to buy new souvenir badges. The price of one souvenir copper badge was said to have been risen by 30 times its original value within one year.

21. China and the Birmingham Mint

The *Hua Qian* is not only found in China. The Birmingham Mint in England once struck a commemorative badge for Luo Fenglu, the Chinese ambassador to England.

Luo, a native of Mingxian County (present-day Minghou) in Fujian Province, served as an interpreter to the Chinese embassy in England as well as France in the early Qing Dynasty. In 1878, the 4th year of the reign of Emperor Guang Xu, he worked as an interpreter in the Chinese embassy in Germany. Later on, he became an aide to Li Hongzhang, prime minister of the Qing government. According to the History of the Qing Dynasty, in 1896, the 22nd year of the reign of Emperor Guang Xu, Luo Fenglu was bestowed the title of the 4th grade official and then appointed ambassador to England, then Italy, and later Belgium. In 1901, the 27th year of the reign of Emperor Guang Xu, he was appointed ambassador to Russia but did not assume the post.

Altogether, Luo worked as an ambassador for five years. It was in 1874, the first year of the reign of Emperor Guang Xu, that the Qing court appointed its first ambassador to station abroad. Mr. Luo was the eighth Chinese ambassador to the United Kingdom.

The work of an ambassador involves international presentations. It could be a matter as important as war and peace as well as seemingly trivial matters of protocol and diplomatic functions. An envoy has to be extremely prudent because his conduct is closely connected with the fate of a state. Zhang Zhitong, governor of Guangdong and Guangxi entrusted Liu Ruifeng, ambassador to England, to purchase a whole set of mint machine tools in 1887, 13th year of the reign of Emperor Guang Xu. Zhang was the first to manufacture silver and copper coins using foreign-bought machine tools. Other provinces followed suit and bought machines to mint silver and copper coins. All those machines were purchased from the famous Birmingham Mint Co., Ltd., in London. In order to learn more about machine tooling, die-making, and to place an order, Luo Fenglu visited the company in January 1900. The Luo Fenglu souvenir badge was a result of his visit.

This badge is 3.9 cm in diameter and 0.25 cm in thickness, weighing 17.7 grams. The obverse has a profile portrait of Luo Fenglu in a long Qing-style gown and characteristic skull cap. The English words on top of the portrait read "Mr. Luo Fenglu" and beneath the portrait "Minister from China." On the reverse, there is a line of words "Visit to Birmingham Mint Co., Ltd. by His Excellency the Chinese Minister." Above the line has the words "for commemoration" while beneath the line "January 1900."

The Birmingham Mint certainly did its homework. They learned about the Chinese *Hua Qian* and had copied its pattern to make the souvenir coin in time for Luo's visit. After a century, however, the Luo Fenglu souvenir badge, its fate unknown, remains only in books.

Chronological Table of Chinese Dynasties

Five August Emperors	c.30th-21st century B.C.
Xia Dynasty	c.21st-16th century B.C.
Shang Dynasty	c.16th-11th century B.C.
Zhou Dynasty	c.11th century-221 B.C.
Western Zhou Dynasty	c.11th century-771 B.C.
Eastern Zhou Dynasty	770-256 B.C.
Spring and Autumn Period	770-476 B.C.
Warring States Period	475-221 B.C.
Qin Dynasty	221-207 B.C.
Han Dynasty	206 B.C.-A.D. 220
Western Han Dynasty	206 B.C.-A.D. 23
Eastern Han Dynasty	A.D. 25-220
Three Kingdoms Period	220-280
Jin Dynasty	265-420
Western Jin Dynasty	265-316
Eastern Jin Dynasty	317-420
Southern and Northern Dynasties	420-589
Sui Dynasty	581-618
Tang Dynasty	618-907
Five Dynasties	907-960
Song Dynasty	960-1279
Northern Song Dynasty	960-1127
Southern Song Dynasty	1127-1279
Liao Dynasty	916-1125
Kin Dynasty	1115-1234
Yuan Dynasty	1271-1368
Ming Dynasty	1368-1644
Qing Dynasty	1644-1911